THE SNAKES CAME BACK

The Snakes Came Back
© 2023 Lora Mathis

ISBN 978-1-988355-36-8
All rights reserved

Published by Metatron Press
Montreal, Quebec
www.metatron.press

Printed in Canada
First printing

Cover Art | Mary Herbert

Library and Archives Canada Cataloguing in Publication
Title: The snakes came back / Lora Mathis.
Names: Mathis, Lora, author.
Identifiers: Canadiana 20230519369 | ISBN 9781988355368 (softcover)
Subjects: LCGFT: Poetry.
Classification: LCC PS3613.A843 S63 2023 | DDC 811/.6—dc23

Metatron Press acknowledges the support of the Canada Council for the Arts.

THE SNAKES CAME BACK

LORA MATHIS

METATRON PRESS

THE SNAKES CAME BACK

LIKE A PRIZE 15
EVERY SOUND IS AN OPENING 16
WHEN I REACH MY BODY 17

DREAM OF THE NEST 21
A GIRL, A BLUR 22
HUMMING DOWNSTAIRS 23

I TOOK YOU 27
DISCLOSURE 28
WHAT CONTINUES TO STICK 30
WHERE THE NOISE COMES FROM 31
DREAM OF UNWANTING 32
A HOOK SLIPS 33

LANGUAGE OF DREAMS 37
BACKDROP OF GREEN LIGHT 38
THE SNAKES CAME BACK 40
THE SUN EATS ITSELF TO SLEEP 42

THE POINT 47
THERE IS NO SMOOTH TRANSITION 48
NOVEMBER 49
NEARBY STORM 50
THERE IS THE FINALITY OF AN END 51
CLEVER MOON 52
ALL WITHOUT 53
ADMISSION 54

SOLITUDE'S REACH 59
NAME FOR A QUICK BEAT 60
F STREET 61
HALTED TIME 63
LUNCH BREAK POEM 64
NO— 65
FANTASY FOR THE TIME 66
CLEAN SLATE 67

THE MEANING OF FIRE 71
WHAT'S IN THE WIND 72
A NOTE 73
MOUSE IN THE HOUSE 74
TOUCH'S SIGNIFICANCE 75
HIGHWAY 1 76
ATTEMPTS TO RID MYSELF OF DESIRE 77

I'LL MELT INTO THE QUIET 81
STRETCHED HEAT 82
SOMETIMES ALL YOU CAN REMEMBER IS THE PHOTOGRAPH 84
THE BAMBOO TREE 85
IF YOU MUST 86

THE COMMITMENT TO CRAFT 91
THE THING IS 92
HAVING A MOMENT 93
WHAT TO DO 94
TALKING SELF-LOVE TONIGHT 95
BORN IN BLOOMINGFOODS 96
SINGING 97
WALKING IN A RED WOOD 98
WATER IS DRAINING FROM MY OLD LIFE 99

NORTH PARK MOON 103
MY DEAR FRIEND 104
CLOAK OF AGING 105
WEEDING THE FAVA BEANS 107
RICH IN THE MORNING 108
SINGLES' DAY 109
SOMEHOW IT RETURNS 110

ATTENTION 115
ANSWERS 116
LET THIS BE 117
THE WAY SOMETIMES 118
IN CELEBRATION 119
ON EARTH 120
TIME PULLED FROM THE MUD 121

What did the sound say to me when we were alone?

Go to the mountain
Don't be afraid

THE SNAKES CAME BACK

LIKE A PRIZE

They say longing like it's a problem
but you love the longing. The longing teaches you.

It shows you a hallway.
You write poems into it.

EVERY SOUND IS AN OPENING

People have been doing this for thousands of years—
Writing poetry, being poets.

We hope our special little names will be noticed
in our life, and beyond, maybe.

Tomorrow is calling out from around the corner.
It cries out again, then pulls its face back towards the wall.

There's no telling which way its voice is coming from.

I'll need to run in every direction,
hoping to catch it before the walls eat it, then me.

WHEN I REACH MY BODY

I will not beg it to come back.

I will write into the stones of it, then skip
them in the sea.

The water writes another story.
Listen:

DREAM OF THE NEST

The bird's wings spread out like a river
winding its tongue through the dirt.

I was a bird, too, flapping my wings in the dark,
watching the story pour by like a film.

While the mothers hunted,
people tore their nests apart,
searching for the babies.

They steered themselves
away from this nest.
They knew better.

I could have watched from overhead.
I could have learned.

Instead, I found myself in this
forbidden place, looking.

Two long writhing snakes hung from her mouth.
They spotted me behind the nest before she did.

Their hisses sucked the air heartily,
Tugging at the gulp in my throat until it burst.

A GIRL, A BLUR

Have you ever been a girl that
explored herself through want?

Legs circling down the back alleys,
fingers letting matches fall in a field.

The neighborhood kids gripped
their bike handlebars and watched.

I was a girl climbing out of my body.
I was a girl who wanted to be a tree.

I climbed my own limbs,
thought if I got high enough, I'd find a way out.

Each time I started climbing, I was called for dinner.
One day, no call came.

I pulled at leaves until I made it past the canopy.
I tugged my own limbs until they burst.

The view did not disappoint.
From the top of the tree, I could see everything.

I looked at the fields and saw
myself, a blur, running.

HUMMING DOWNSTAIRS

It was twilight. My mother was humming downstairs.
I learned how to walk so I could reach her.
I swayed on carpeted stairs.

When I fell, her singing caught me.
She said, *When you were a child, you cried so much.*
I had to keep going upstairs to console you.

Now I rush down the stairs in the home I live in
with five roommates.
Night twists in. My legs will not work like they used to.

I walk and I fall. I fall and I wait for singing.
When I get up, my own voice finds me.
I keep looking for you, until I reach a mirror.

I TOOK YOU

into the green square of my heart
to devour you.
You live inside my tiny head now.

We slice pomegranates with our teeth.
Lap up pools from desire's wet mouth.

There it is, just stirring a bit—
the thing that continues once the body
has been wiped away.

DISCLOSURE

It is a fine date.

> Conversations carried to background harmonies.
> A bowl of popcorn pawed at.
> Three drinks and a second pillow pulled
> from the closet under moonlight.

Still, dawn cradles the question of running.

> Shall I throw myself into the morning
> while you lie there sleeping,
> your breath steady and oblivious?

If you lie naked inside me I will blend you into every other who has been positioned on top of me.

> Bodies melting into one mound of flesh,
> slithering swiftly through the grass.
> The rush of them stirring the blades into shaking.

How I will resent you,
>oblivious stranger,
>as I lie alone in my bed
>the following morning.

Oh, it's not you,
                but the nature of the night
                which makes the fields shudder.

                Don't touch me.
                My skin is made of snakes.

WHAT CONTINUES TO STICK

He is playing the same bars,
hosting parties with the same friends attending,
probably still fingering the small white pills
as he tells someone how much he has read about war.

While I am here, in a city he has not visited,
writing poems.

My name—a night ruiner, not to be spoken
at the bar, avoided in conversation
with his new girlfriend. Small banishment.

This is the truth I keep getting stuck on.

How he can continue without interruption,
while I am a river whose loss built
a whole new canyon in the mountain of myself.

Now, in the stillness of my bedroom,
surrounded by things I accumulated after knowing him,
wearing clothes he has never seen me in,
I am still stuck—nails deep,
scraping the thick gum off my shoes.

WHERE THE NOISE COMES FROM

Our 30 seconds of small talk are a half-inflated balloon
floating towards the ceiling.
One flick of my tongue and I could pop it,
but I keep my carefully sharpened teeth
good and nice in my mouth.

I imagine smashing a glass into the wall
while staring straight at him. I imagine screaming
in his face, demanding he leave.

The music stopping.
      The laughter filtering out.
           The fear spreading across my friends' faces.

I want to ruin his night, but instead I smile.
A minute later he is in another conversation,
cracking open his sixth beer.

The snap of the pull tab reverberates like a giggle.
It jolts into my body until I can't distinguish

      what of me is skin and what is noise.

           The entire room is buzzing.
           I feel his laughter everywhere.

DREAM OF UNWANTING

The stranger sobs with a gun in his mouth
while Rivka cracks pistachios with their tongue, bored.

Somehow we're all in the apartment
my mom lost her hair in,
and the sobber has the face of the man who ignored
the meeting in my ears to insist

I smell his pride,
that jar of rich and earthy weed.

What, to these men, do I represent?
Shadowy thing, half inked idea of want.

If they were writing the story, my mention of a boyfriend
would crawl back into my mouth.

Still this cloudy haze could settle the same—
The gun screaming at the ceiling while paint
fell on the nut shells at our feet.

A HOOK SLIPS

With his tongue in my mouth,
I feel akin to a caught fish.

When his fingers move to my nipple,
squeezing hard, the hook slips into my mouth.

I fix my eyes on the houses in front of us, their
alert gaze lit up under the afternoon sunlight.

His tongue becomes a blade, preparing
to gut me, and I start writing this poem in my head:

Here is my way out. My escape
from floundering on the hull,
wishing for water.

In it, I exist elsewhere. I course through the lake and emerge
dripping with light. Spilled free of touch.

LANGUAGE OF DREAMS

A snake slithers into a dream.
Bites off its own head, then grows a new one.

Last night, two snakes dangled
from a massive bird's mouth.
The night before, a giant bird perched
upon a decrepit warehouse.

What does the language of dreams
wish to explain?

A friend becomes a predator.
A stranger who demanded my number
sobs in my father's armchair.
We take selfies to see how hideous we've become,
while a green light unfurls through the window.

Look: Morning is coming in.
Watch it fall apart. Watch the dreams
devour it, and leave a green film behind.

BACKDROP OF GREEN LIGHT

Water leaps across the trees' faces. Shriber's spotting.
Mine is green-tipped bones behind grass blades.
All of ours': stumps devoured by beaks.

What lies beneath the surface, just close enough,
to make you hammer against a barrier and search?

Salt smell slips out of green marsh, bright green
like the dream where the sky ripped in half

like it was a piece of paper, flimsy, shreddable,
a set collapsing mid-performance.

This was not a dream, the smell of salt air tangible,
the power lines cutting across the hot wind,

Hunt's voice saying, *We can't look at anything
without ourselves in it.*

Here I am in it, intruding,
looking at a power plant behind sliced down trees.

Come night I bash my legs against a metal table,
I plead with unfazed nurses, I give an attitude, I reach

for my phone, searching
for directions out of dreaming.

In the morning waking feels wider, uncertain,
like it is cloaked in green light.

Walking again on hard dirt, Mando and I plot
a radio novella beside still water.

We sing the notes of a piano trailing down the keys,
we try on the voices of nurses, back and forth,

no there should not be so much of a conversation,
to make it believable the nurses have to go along

with their work unfazed,
they have to slice the sky in two.

So when we look around we question waking,
we wonder what lies beneath the surface of a day,

we reach out to touch the green morning
and expect it to fall apart in our hands.

THE SNAKES CAME BACK

Consider a spotlight. Point it to the grass.
There, where the two snakes are winding together.

Their bodies luminous, like thread, stitched in and out.
Scales looping into one song.

Cut!

Two women sit across a plastic table and slip off jealousy.
One says, I too walked through the night and did not return.

Cut!

While standing in your dad's kitchen waiting
for the kettle to scream,
I see two snakes weaving through the dry grass.
Their scales winding together in the lush moonlight.
The blue clouds pregnant with flames.

Cut!   *Cut!*   *Cut!*

Cut! cut!
         Cut!
         Cut!
       Cut!
     Cut!
  CUT
  Cut!
       Cut!
          Cut!
            Cut
          Cut
      CUT
    Cut!

The snakes came back last night.

I tried to feed them street names, corners
we'd stopped on. They slid through
the grass, refusing to look at me.

To drive in the direction of the past.
To listen to the kettle calling and hear only hissing.

THE SUN EATS ITSELF TO SLEEP

This is not my home.
It is a body.

I found it on the ground
and slipped it on.

I live here now.

THE POINT

Men fall away from me like leaves.

On the phone, my mother cites
the difficulties of my childhood as a reason

I'm tougher.
This is the point we've gotten to—

the flu medicine dissolving into liquid
under my tongue, her dogs barking
at imagined strangers at the door.

The men we've loved somewhere else.

TV noise buzzing in their ears
like flies.

THERE IS NO SMOOTH TRANSITION

into loss.
A month ago he and I
shared a bed together and
spoke of trips we wanted to take.
Now we text while I'm on a plane home, alone.
He's sorry for letting me down.
There's not much to say.
I read the clear black letters on the screen
and imagine the love we have for one another
as a separate being, growing out of its skin.
Its fervent eyes watching.
The whole night existing in its mouth.

NOVEMBER

In the morning I pace down
to the garden, look around.

Some nights my ex comes over,
just to hold me,

then I inspect his Tinder profile with him.

I get the feeling I have been alive for too long
and then barely anything–

a blink.

I close my eyes to clear the dust of the day
then my whole life is gone.

NEARBY STORM

We used to climb over this city together.
Today the clouds grew heavy as we sat on the rocky ground,

swapping post-break up admissions,
the last of the day dissolving.

When we got to the bottom of the hill,
the air was clear but the ground was wet.

On the drive back—silence.
Until more confessions, a steady pouring,

a nearby storm spreading
across your car windows. I fell asleep

with the windows open then woke to rain
coursing through my dreams.

THERE IS THE FINALITY OF AN END

and then there is this:
dishes falling over each other on the rack,

tomato paste streaked in the pot. The day still sucking
in gulps of cold, firm air as the clock ticks

on the wall. The reminder of the past
an imprint, stuck in the yellow

light soaking the walls
while the kettle screams in the corner.

CLEVER MOON

I'm sad again, what is there to say of it?
Again, the moon is buoyant in the sky.
The car creaking down the 5,
the silence directing me forward.
This night is not new.
I have lived it many times.
On this freeway, coming from a show,
a sadness lingering on the fray.
Again, the passing road work steam.
The red light slick on the road.
And this immovable, clever, clever moon.

ALL WITHOUT

The world is coated in love and then it isn't again.
The birds sing their songs the same as they have.
The bats sailing through the night are still directioned and screeching.
The possum strutting across the fence line still turns
its yellow eyes to me and roars.
The stream in the park still flows forward.
Is this not all a display of love?

<blockquote>
Oh, be in love with me or don't.
My day does not depend on it.
</blockquote>

ADMISSION

You have let me go even as you are texting me
that maybe we can talk about things later on.

I am letting you go, too,
bursting the admission against the wind,
allowing it to splinter out of me.

I don't have you—
well, I don't want this grief either.

Now there is so much rich emptiness
I swear the wind runs through it for hours
without reaching an end.

SOLITUDE'S REACH

is limitless.

Today I want to call all of my friends.
Mouth, I love you into the phone.

Gestures to cross the bridge of alienation.

Oh we're all alone in our bedrooms now,
staring out at deep skies and yawning.

NAME FOR A QUICK BEAT

Sitting on the asphalt listening
to the rhythm of my neighbor dribbling
after being slapped in the face with virus headlines.

The headlines list the daily death counts climbing.
150,000 dead, and rising.

My neighbor dribbles faster and faster,
his basketball rhythm becoming a hum.

F STREET

It is week three of being physically distanced.
The days blur together, become a foggy monotony.

Everyday I try to take a walk or ride my bike,
something to get the blood moving, to remind myself

of natal plums, loquats, the food
that can be foraged in my neighborhood.

Today a BMX biker circled me,
he was on every street I turned,

jumping off a curb or careening
towards me on the sidewalk.

Ten minutes later my headphones filled
the empty streets with promises of better days.

Then there he was again: slapping my ass,
his bike a haze,

almost out of sight
as I shouted, *Fuck you!*

Anger bursts out of me.

I can't contain its blaze.

At home I collapse on my bed,
the fire splintering into grief.

HALTED TIME

I don't have time to be angry today.
There are too many books I would like to read,
poems I have yet to write, deadlines clucking
loudly in my ear.

I don't have time to be angry.
I need to make the bed, bleach the sink,
pour oil into the pan and watch it snarl.

But I am still mad, furious and biting,
seething around the clock
smashed to bits on the floor.

LUNCH BREAK POEM

File your taxes.
        Apply to schools.

Check your bank balance, again.
                      Oh! Rent is due.

Have you thought about getting someone to share your room?
        Have you thought about leaving California?
           Have you been making art lately?

The best artists find the time.
The best artists make it happen!

                What do you *mean* you're tired all the time?

Have you thought about taking vitamins have you thought about working harder have you thought about blocking your friends' numbers have you thought about sleeping in your car to avoid traffic

    Oh! You're five minutes over your break and rent is due.

No I will not answer your email rapidly.
No I will not continue to be an excellent employee.
No I will not be going out tonight.
No I will not leave this bed until I feel like it.
No I will not be able to give you a set answer.
No I will not be attending your livestream–

    I'm sorry.
    There's so much dirt for my hands to disappear in,
    and so much to scream about.

FANTASY FOR THE TIME

There will be a time when I sit with someone else in a room and our hands touch.
>Filthy fantasy. Sordid for the time.
>Porn of two people in hazmat suits, grinding.

When did outside become a question?
Now we argue online over whether it is acceptable to take a daily walk.

A man bikes up behind me to slap my ass as if to say,
>*Let this terror drive you inside.*

I'm gonna make a soup tonight.
Throw four different types of vegetables in.
Even add some lentils.
There will be no rationing
the amount of items I can use in this meal.
>Gonna slurp it up like tomorrow is a regular old day.

>I'm luxuriating in my own fear.
>Doing backstroke laps in a pool of complete dread.

CLEAN SLATE

Rain has been droning all day.
Endless pouring, and I keep writing

the same words: *I'm alone again*—
as if they'll jump from the page, grow a mouth.

I want to delete my social media until January,
dive into the new year with a clean slate.

But there's no need for a cryptic post before
doing so, the final wave from the boat's edge.

The old dog is pacing in the kitchen.
He crashes into tables, gets stuck in the table's legs.

In my arms he's all bones and my mom says,
What do you want me to do? He wants to live.
as the rain bleats on.

THE MEANING OF FIRE

In the cool blue blaze, I am driving home.
The meal still in my stomach, the full day yawning into night.

Two or three nights a week I share dinner
with you and your dad. Tacos, pizza, something simple.

Once the plates are cleared I help spoon applesauce
and crushed meds into your mouth.

This is no longer shapeless grief, but habit.
The way life transforms once loss has settled.

Through my windshield I watch the clouds darken
to shadow as the moon gleams above,

its proud hands spread across its belly,
so large and brilliant as it settles into the flames.

WHAT'S IN THE WIND

Here it comes again, the talk of perseverance
once the days grow longer.
Mockingbirds tussle on the power line, fighting for space,
their songs interrupted by shrill squawks.

I am starting to see there is as much violence
in survival as there is beauty.

For now, I am studying the wind.
How it transforms from breeze to gust.
How much power it holds even while murmuring.

I want to be like that: unwieldy and sweeping.
I want to pass through everything.

A NOTE

Gnaw your way out of loss.
Endure the burning.

The aloneness is stifling at times—
how far it can spread.

Find the fracture,
or let the wound breathe.

Not everything must be processed, parceled,
and healed in an instant.

MOUSE IN THE HOUSE

November again, all alone!
No noise in the house, the bed
cold. No one to talk to, no one
to hold! The hours spilling
out and nothing to do but
laugh and grow old!

TOUCH'S SIGNIFICANCE

After three months of not being touched,
when I go to do it myself,
my fingers grow bored with the movements.

A splendid dance is erupting in the trees.
Here is the hunger I placed aside.

Let my want flutter quickly across the stage.
Let it bring rain licking at the trees.

HIGHWAY 1

There is no need to fuck someone.
Spend the day in the car, windows down.
Sit on the porch 'til the sky dives into pink.
Watch the cows grazing in front of you
as you devour olives from the jar,
Sucking them off your fingers,
working the pits around your tongue,
whittling them down like the hungry bitch you are.

ATTEMPTS TO RID MYSELF OF DESIRE

Bashing my guitar for hours, making a spell
of the same chords, breathing in
saltwater, rubbing it into my hair,
sucking down passionfruit over the sink,
dancing alone as the eggs cook,
reading poetry to the birds,
drinking cool water in a warm shower.

>Cool naked body.
>>Warm naked body.
>>>Body in bed listening to the trees.
>>>>Body sweating out the ocean.

The ocean's mouth slips open, widens into a wave.

Here, a way to be devoured–
To be totally consumed then slip out on another side.

I'LL MELT INTO THE QUIET

and become it.
I'll take off my skin and sprout a new one.

STRETCHED HEAT

In this city of stretched heat
I, freshly licensed, drive myself

down the boulevards
we used to cruise together.

In this home I have returned to, this city
whose stillness once felt stagnant, I move slowly.

I take myself to the gym,
write music in a hot garage,

dig my roots further
into this parched earth.

My eyes catch sight of your tags
on surrounding rooftops

on my drive to your dad's.
There, on warm days, your partner wheels you

into the backyard,
where we sit with eyes closed.

Now in Oregon, I drive down the street we used to live on.
I nod at your initials hovering above the freeway.

Time has not made this wound any smaller.
Life has not shrunk this grief.

In Portland, I wake up on Wren's couch
to a dream of you laughing,

and I want so badly to be moving
deep into the day together.

Instead I throw myself down the streets
we went down quick together

and I do not ask myself
where I am going.

Today, the destination holds no weight.
My only focus is moving.

I am moving into the boundless sky
that holds no mention of endings.

I am going as far as it takes.

SOMETIMES ALL YOU CAN REMEMBER IS THE PHOTOGRAPH

The memory becomes it. Other details become fuzzy. They fall away. The memory becomes still, like it was in the photo. It is contained in the frame. I can only remember the place we stopped on the trestle, taking off layers and walking across the wood, eating peanut butter and jelly sandwiches under the hot sun. But I don't remember the way there, or the way back. Only the photographed moment.

THE BAMBOO TREE

Yesterday, unwillingly hunched over the toilet,
my body rejected whatever I tried to nurture it with.

Sometimes the body pushes itself to a screaming halt,
gives a push to go slower, to not force anything.

After leaving the bathroom,
I stood on the balcony, focusing on the blue
spreading across the bamboo tree.

The day's mouth is foaming.
It bleeds at the gums.

There is no resisting slowness anymore.
Sit in the garden, turn off the phone,

drink a cup of tea when the stomach has calmed,
and watch the bamboo leaves settle
into deep blue night.

IF YOU MUST

Reduce life to one long, vivid letting go,
go ahead.

Sure, joy slips out the window,
but why shiver each time it goes?

Leave the window wide.
Flip the kettle on and let the night air throw itself in
while awaiting joy's return.

THE COMMITMENT TO CRAFT

My laughter is my craft.
The way I kiss is my craft.
The meal we're sharing is my craft.
How I listen is my craft.
Every day I am honing my craft.
Sloughing off all language is my craft.
I practice my craft in the grocery store aisles.
I practice my craft in bed, with your face pressed into my shoulder.
Every walk I go on is a cultivation of my craft.
Every plot of dirt I've plopped down on has been a studio.
In each second of being, I am honing my craft.
I am sharpening the body of it until it cuts the air.

THE THING IS

You read some poets' words and think,
No one has ever understood me like this.
They must be my soulmate!
A genius! They really understand!

Then you get into a room with them
where they're sitting wearing an old sweatshirt
with a tomato stain down the front of it.

What do we expect from these people?
They stare at the sky for an hour
only to run home whispering,

I was a cloud. I was a cloud
Until I melted away.

HAVING A MOMENT

Staring at myself in the mirror, I start granting forgiveness
to things which never asked for it.

Fake potted plant with leaves coated in dust, I forgive you.
Paper towels threatening to litter the ground, I forgive you.

Mirror's reflection, uncomfortable and refusing to
meet my eyes, I forgive.

There is hardly a romance in this.
I forgive.
I kick at the dirt on the floor.
I forgive.
Rub my finger over the plastic plant's leaf and note the dust.
I forgive.

Someone knocks and asks if I will be long.
I forgive you, I whisper.

Outside a voice says,
Hello? I really gotta go.

WHAT TO DO

Cook a meal, or go to sleep.
Walk until your ankles bleed.
Read a poem, or make the bed.
Kiss your lover on the head.
Fold the laundry, pay the rent.
Wish for the money you've spent.
Run a mile, collapse in steam.
Course the needle through a seam.
Sit in silence or drive all night.
Eat an apple, say goodbye!

TALKING SELF-LOVE TONIGHT

Listen up, little bitch
                      I whisper to the mirror.

I'm going to love you, cook you dinner,
take you on a bike ride, rub your hair
when your worry is set off.

      I know it's *often*.
      You say that like I'll get tired. But I won't.

           I'm a pit of inexhaustible care.
           The void looks into me and I laugh.

      You want love?
      Care so pure you could drink it?

           I'll give you it by the bottle.
           Refill your glass and keep pouring.

BORN IN BLOOMINGFOODS

I stood in the orange co-op bathroom for a very long time.
My body and I taking each other in, two unsure animals
trying to determine if the other was a predator.

Then the laughter spilled
out of me. I was swimming in it.

My body was doing laps in laughter.
We embraced like long time friends
finally returning to each other.

SINGING

The shyness of my heart asks me who I am
to share these poems.
To take these quiet thoughts—which we all have—
and press them into books.

Then, something stiller and immovable
in me answers,

We are all singing praises to the world
in different ways. This is just my song.

WALKING IN A RED WOOD

I stitched a garland of questions.
I wore it around my neck with pride.
I adopted fool as my new name.
I ate my own heart out on the living room floor.
I made a meal of my upset hunger.
I went walking in a red wood.
I made peace with the heart's dragon.
I tamed my own head with rosemary and wood shavings.
I made a fire of the ladder I was laying at heaven's door.
Now I'll never be cold again.

WATER IS DRAINING FROM MY OLD LIFE
Poem by predictive text

The snakes have been such a blessing in the past.
The two women are in the center for the last night.

To be here for the first time.
To write it down for the next time.

We don't have to read
all these years of life in a row.

NORTH PARK MOON

Watching my friend catch tags,
uncapped flick of a pen quick,

then back in the pocket.
The legs already moving on.

Tonight the fog was thick enough
that the years muddled together.

Keeping watch, my eyes hugging the night,
this could be another year.

The palm trees arching over our heads can't tell.
The chipped asphalt doesn't care either way.

The half moon lighting the sidewalk is unconcerned
with pocket-sized ideas of time.

It beams through the thicket as it always has,
pointing out the fallen plumerias on our path.

MY DEAR FRIEND,

Again we have forgotten
to leave the candle out tonight.

If you forget your way,
Will you come to my window?

I've kept the brightest flower
in the tree for you.

CLOAK OF AGING

While staying in the apartment of two friends,
I remained in the same mile radius.

Slipped out to the grocery store across the street
and came back to quietly chop

potatoes and onions, so when they woke up
there would be a meal to share.

I can sense my grandmothers' capabilities inside me
while my hands work over the food.

Returning to when I'd shuck corn with her
while French radio cooed in the background.

We would spend afternoons in Montréal
pulling cobweb coating

from the yellow kernels, our hands tangled
in thin white strings.

A few years later, back with my mother,
I bound up the familiar stairs first.

The door opened to reveal the smell of onions
and a distant swooping of the radio.

Cloaked in the haze of aging,
my grandmother squinted at me in confusion,
for a second uncertain of who I was,

but still asking,

Tu veux manger?

WEEDING THE FAVA BEANS

Hands work the soil, digging up the Bermuda grass,
and bits of last year's tomatoes.

Jack points out the not yet blooming poppies,
and I move around their jagged leaves.

In the summer there will be salads with fava flowers
and muffins sprinkled with poppy seeds.

For now, under the noonday sun, we work—
backs arched, fingers plunged into the dirt,
making room for the coming meals.

RICH IN THE MORNING

> *In this world I am as rich as I need to be*
> – Mary Oliver

I am rich, and my friends are rich with me
cuz we climb on desert boulders
to take in the blood red tongue of the sun
licking at the rocky hills.

We are rich, standing before the eclipsed moon
and howling from our chests.

We are rich, making a game of tossing
broken limestone onto a rusted pole in the center,
our eyes clinging to each falling rock as it moves
towards the mossy floor, as concentrated
as if this game determined the state of our lives.

We are rich, for we take in the world, and don't believe
we are ever able to own it, nor desire to.

We are rich as we stand together before the wetlands,
gazing at the reeds which swallow poisons then exhale
clean, deep air, our muddy boots heavy upon us,
content to simply look at the world together and laugh.

SINGLES' DAY

It's 11/11, Singles Day', or so the email
asking me to buy sweaters says.

This I relay to the two friends I am
moving through Balboa Park with.

They're not impressed.
I don't want to be single!, one says. The other laughs.

I've kissed them both.
Made a home with one of them.

Now we travel under the eucalyptuses,
sipping up the silence between us,

stomachs full of fries,
the sound of the wheelchair

running over the
sidewalk cracks while they whisper,

We have each other. That's better,
I take my turn pushing the chair

and think,
Oh yes, it's true.

SOMEHOW IT RETURNS

The thing I was out looking for,
what I thought was lost and irrecoverable.

I found it plainly: while chopping mushrooms
in your dad's kitchen,
waiting for the oil to heat behind me.

I was making our lunch, and you called to me
from the next room, asking for a glass of water.

There is loss, but there is renewal too.
I hand you the glass, drop some garlic into the pan.

Once you were my partner, now you are my friend.
Once you cooked me lasagna

while I was sick from my own head.
Now I bring you crushed Tylenol and tacos.

What I thought I lost irrecoverably
has come back

so quiet and plainly
that I wonder if it ever left.

ATTENTION

There is only one way.

When I thought there were many,
I wondered which path to take.

Now I see the larger path
laid out around all of them.

I can only walk in love
through shadows of uncertainty,
or I cannot walk at all.

ANSWERS

What I care to say is simple. Watch the waves
while seated on a rock, slip into the ocean's mouth,
then find your perch and do it again.

A whole life could be lived this way.
Studying, observing, looking around.

The water, the pelicans, seagulls with beakfuls of scrap feast–
there is an entire world to be a student of. Delight in it.

One could spend their whole life searching
for truths held in the conversation
the world is having every day.

LET THIS BE

Sun spilling across the countertop.
Chicken coop littered with orange peels.
Street cat basking under the bamboo.

Banana trees outside my window thrashing
to some song

I can't hear. I couldn't sing.
But I dance along to all the same.

THE WAY SOMETIMES

The way sometimes a moment is so sacred
you don't want to speak about it.

Even in the intimacy of bed, language acts as a pin
trying to still the wings of a butterfly,
still singing of flight.

No, you want to keep it tucked inside your pocket
like a piece of sea glass

you can rub your thumb over to remind you,
life is impossible and real.

IN CELEBRATION

When the day is long.
When the historians wag their fingers in warning.
When the browned water serves fish belly-up, cross-eyed.
When the bees cease their buzzing about.
When the heart once carved smooth welds into a knife.
When the mirror's reflection holds no intimacy.
When the soft stillness of a room grows suffocating.
When the night has no more answers than the day.
When you believe yourself incapable of even a step further,
will you celebrate with me still?

Even in the blaze of unrelenting living
will you throw up your feet and with me,
feel the sheer luck we are swaying on?

ON EARTH

The body contemplates purpose.
Meanwhile, the spirit takes a nap.

The body considers word choices and life paths
while the spirit yawns in the sun.

From its corner, the body pouts and insists
the years must be accounted for.

In its palm, time is a gap
that's closing,

but the spirit throws its head
to the wind without hurry.

It has looked out at time's expanse.
It already knows it's infinite.

TIME PULLED FROM THE MUD

Sometimes it only takes the cold air to bring you back
to the warm light on the dirt road,
your grandmother calling from the kitchen,
the radio pouring down the hallway as she falls asleep.

You pull time out from the mud.
You wrap it around your wrist.
You live all over again.

NOTES

"Dream of the Nest" was written in response to a prompt by C.S. Giscombe to describe a dream.

"A Girl, A Blur" was written after reading Yena Sharma Purmasir's *VIRAHA*, which I was lucky to blurb.

"Humming Downstairs" is for my mom, as is so much in this book and in what I make.

An early version of "What Continues to Stick" was published in ÖMËGÄ in 2016.

"Dream of Unwanting" was written in response to a sonnet prompt by C.S. Giscombe.

"Backdrop of Green Light" was written in response to a prompt by C.S. Giscombe to write a haibun that weaves in a dream.

"The Snakes Came Back" was published, digitally and in print, in *Spectra Poets 2*.

An early version of "The Sun Eats Itself to Sleep" was also published, in print, in *Spectra Poets 2*. A spoken word version of the poem is featured on the track "Memories End" off the album *Boxer* by The Egg Factory. This poem was also written in response to a prompt by C.S. Giscombe.

"Lunch Break Poem" was turned into the pop spoken word track "Rent Is Due" with Gonzalo Meza.

"No–" was featured in the experimental essay *Here I Am In It*, published by Burn All Books in 2022.

"The Thing Is" was published, in print and digitally, in *Spectra Poets 2*.

"Water is Draining From My Old Life" was written using the predictive text feature on my iPhone. I would prompt the feature by beginning a sentence, then follow it to an end. Editing occurred in the ordering of phrases, but not in the words themselves.

"Cloak of Aging" is for my grandmother, as are so many of these poems.

"Weeding the Fava Beans" is for Jack Kellner.

"Rich in the Morning" has an epitaph from a Mary Oliver. "In this world, I am as rich as I need to be" is from her poem "Winter," as featured in *New and Selected Poems Volume 1*. The poem is dedicated to Chance Newell and Chris Eugene.

"Singles' Day" is dedicated to Chris Eugene and Matt Swanguen.

"Somehow It Returns" is dedicated to Matt Swanguen, as is so much of this book. It was made while listening to Arthur Russell's song "Love Comes Back," off the album *Love Is Overtaking Me*, on repeat.

"In Celebration" was performed as part of Angel Acuña's choreographed piece "Celebration" for San Diego's 2019 Trolley Dances. Participating in that performance and learning from the group was a wonderful experience. Reciting my poem aloud multiple times a day, for two weeks, while wearing an all silver mylar outfit, changed the poem and me.

Many of these poems were first performed in a collaborative set with musician Matty Terrones. A number of these poems can be found on our collaborative spoken word album *Sediment*, from the label Hello America Stereo Cassette.

The title of this book is my handwriting.

The symbol separating each section is the alchemical symbol for "hour."

The font for this book is Garamond.

ACKNOWLEDGEMENTS

Thank you to the editors and artists who gave a home to early versions of these poems. Thank you to all who have booked and attended shows I have participated in, and given me a chance to sort through these poems in front of an audience. Special thanks to all involved with Verbatim Books, the Brown Building, and the Ché Café in San Diego. Thank you to Burn All Books.

Thank you to Matty Terrones, for being a longtime friend and for collaborating with me to create immersive worlds of poetry and sound. Walking through these poems with you is a dream.

Thank you to Zane Alexander for recording the spoken word album *Sediment*, and to Adam Gnade for giving many of these poems an audio home before they were a part of this book. Thank you Edgar Alejandre for inviting me to be a part of your album. Thank you Angel Acuña, and the rest of the dancers in your piece, for believing in my work and inviting me to be a part of yours.

Thank you to Metatron Press for giving this book a home. Thank you Ashley Obscura for caring so deeply about the work, and for your stewardship in making this book alive. Thank you to Hannah Karpinksi for writing a press release about the work.

Thank you Mary Herbert for the use of your pastel drawing on the cover. It is an honor.

Thank you to those that blurbed this book: Amy Berkowitz, Adam Gnade, and Erin Taylor.

Thank you to my teachers for shaping and sharpening me. Kelly Mayhew and Jim Miller, your love of words, dedication to your students, and now, your friendship, has guided me. Cecil Giscombe, thank you for the encouragement to give weight to our dreams. You, and my former classmates, were incredible teachers in poetry.

Poems are lived before, and as they are written. Thank you to the many who have helped me live through these poems. The conversations we've had, walks we've taken, trips we've gone on, and tables we've sat around together are where these poems are born from.

Thank you to my family—to my mom, my sister, my brother, and my grandmother. You have all taught me the importance of humor, dedication, and not getting stuck in the mud for too long.

Thank you to the many at La Querencia and for the conversations—some several hours long, some five minutes—that molded these poems.

Thank you to Matt Swanguen. How to find the words for the weird ways life changes us? I'm glad to be your friend through it all.

Thank you John Swanguen for showing me how to go through change with care.

Thank you to: Isaiah Acosta, Brianna Arellano-Meli, Lolly Beck-Pancer, Ameen Beydoun, Andrea Carter, Barbara Durazo, Chris Eugene, Nature Fejerang, Robi Foli, Chris Giuffre, Leah Levinson, Rebecca Jones, Gonzalo Meza, Cecilia Mignon, Terra Oliveira, Rachel Petitt, Trina Pham, David Reyes, Pedro Rolón, Matty Terrones, Jenny Yang, and Rivka Yeker. I am better for your wisdom and humor.

Thank you to Armando Resendez for your patience, and for being of love. I am so glad to be in this with you.

Thank you to the trees, the weeds, and the animals.

Thank you to the ghosts, to my grandparents and Ariel. I hope you are resting easy.

Thank you, dear reader.

LORA MATHIS

Photo by Trina Pham

Lora Mathis is a poet and artist who grew up between Southern California and Québec. They enjoy bouncing between mediums, and work in video, photography, graphic design, sculpture, printmaking, and performance. Their first full-length collection of poems, *The Women Widowed to Themselves* was originally published by Where Are You Press in 2015, and republished by Party Trick Press in 2020. They perform poetry on their own, and with their frequent sound collaborator, Matty Terrones. Mathis is a graduate of UC Berkeley, and currently lives in Oakland.

www.loramathis.com
Instagram: @lora__mathis